I0705776

Throne of Windsor

Frederick Oscar

Copyright © Frederick Oscar 2022

All Rights Reserved

Table of content

PREFACE

The history of the late monarch Elizabeth II and her Successor, and in particular, her early years and ascent to power, has recently attracted new interest.

By highlighting choices made by earlier members of the great royal family that may have directly or indirectly led to the current monarchs of our time, this book seeks to address some of the fundamental questions that have plagued royal family admirers and the inquisitive minds of millions of men and women about the Windsor royal family.

I'd want to thank everyone who read the manuscripts and provided helpful critique. As a result, I have no qualms about praising the significance of this book.

Part 1

George V

George Frederick Ernest Albert, who was born on June 3, 1865 served as Emperor of India from May 6, 1910, until his death. George, the second child of Albert Edward, Prince of Wale, came behind his father and older brother, Prince Albert Victor, in the line of succession to the British crown. George Frederick Ernest Albert, who lived from 3 June 1865 to 20 January 1936, served as Emperor of India from 6 May 1910 until his death in 1936. He also served as King of the United Kingdom and the British Domains.

George came behind his elder brother, Prince Albert Victor, and his father in the line of succession to the British throne. Prince George spent several years serving under his uncle, Prince Alfred, Duke of Edinburgh, as a young man in the naval force. There, he became close to and completely smitten with his cousin, Princess Marie of Edinburgh. Grandma, dad, and uncle all backed his decision to date her, but his mother and aunts, the Princess of Wales and Maria Alexandrovna, Duchess of Edinburgh, condemned the pairing. The Duchess of Edinburgh hated Britain, and the Princess of Wales thought the family was overly pro-German. Albert Victor, George's older brother, proposed to his second cousin Princess Victoria Mary of Teck, often referred to as "May," in November 1891. Her parents were Princess Mary Adelaide of Cambridge, a male-line descendant of George III and a first cousin of Queen Victoria, and

Francis, Duke of Teck, a member of a morganatic, cadet branch of the House of Württemberg.

Albert Victor passed away from pneumonia during a flu pandemic on January 14, 1892, just a month and a half after the proper engagement, placing George second in line to the throne and likely to succeed his Father. Typhoid fever, the ailment that is rumored to have killed George's great-grandfather Prince Albert, had kept him confined to bed for a considerable amount of time. George had just about recovered from this severe illness. George and Princess May grew close during their shared period of loss because Queen Victoria saw May as a reasonable equivalent for her grandson. George got May's approval for his marriage proposal one year after Albert Victor's death. On July 6, 1893, they exchanged vows in the Sanctuary Imperial at London's St. James's Palace. They were committed to one another throughout their entire lives. Despite the fact that George claimed he was unable to express his feelings well in conversation, they frequently exchanged cherished letters and charming notes.

King Edward VIII was the first of George V's six children, followed by King George VI, Princes Mary, Princess Royal and Countess of Harewood, Prince Henry, Duke of Gloucester, Prince George, Duke of Kent and Prince John of the United Kingdom, who is the fifth. Randolph Churchill confirmed that George was a strict father who made his children uncomfortable, and that George had spoken to the Earl of Derby: "My father was terrified of his mother, I was terrified of my father, and I'm going to hell and high water make sure that my kids are terrified of me. There isn't a hotspot for the citation right away, and it's likely that George's nurturing approach wasn't quite the same as what many people were doing at the time. Whether or not this was the case, his children seemed to detest his strict demeanor, with Prince Henry trying to portray him as a dreadful father in later years.

George V spent the majority of his early years as the Duke of York at York Cottage, a modest home in Sandringham, Norfolk, where their way of life reflected that of a pleasant working-class family rather than that of a monarch. In contrast to his father's active public pursuits, George preferred a basic, essentially peaceful lifestyle. Throughout his tenure as Duke of York. By any stretch of the imagination, all he did was shoot things and stamp them. George was a passionate stamp collector who played a significant role in transforming the Imperial Philatelic Collection into the largest collection of British and Commonwealth stamps in the history of the world, sometimes by setting record prices for individual items. In his capacity as Duke of York, George fulfilled a variety of civic duties. After Queen Victoria died on January 22, 1901, George's Father ascended to the throne as King Edward VII. George was given the title of Duke of Cornwall; for the majority of the remaining months of that year, The Duke of Cornwall and York was his title.

Upon the creation of the Commonwealth of Australia, the Duke declared open the main session of the Australian Parliament. He praised the tactical abilities, bravery, loyalty, and duty to duty of New Zealanders there, and the visit gave New Zealand a chance to show off its support, notably in its adoption of cutting-edge English principles in correspondences and the running of enterprises. The specific goal was to highlight New Zealand's appealing qualities to tourists and prospective settlers while avoiding awareness of emerging social tensions by focusing the British press on areas that few people were aware of.

In a speech at Guildhall in London on his return to Britain, George issued a warning about "the impression which appeared to win among [our] Brothers across the seas, the Old Nation should awaken if she is to maintain her previous position of dominance in her colonial commerce despite new rivals. On November 9th, 1901, George was created Prince of Wales and Earl of Chester. King Edward wanted to prepare his son for his upcoming throne. George was allowed full access to state archives by his father, unlike Edward, who Queen Victoria had specifically forbidden from participating in governmental activities. George consequently gave his better half access to his papers. He valued her opinion, and she often recalled her significant other's speeches. As Prince of Wales, he supported improvements in maritime training, such as enlisting recruits at the ages of twelve and thirteen and providing them with the same education regardless of their class and potential jobs. The modifications were made by Sir John Fisher, then Second (and subsequently First) Sir Lord. George and May traveled to British India between November 1905 and March 1906. While there, he was horrified by racial segregation and pushed for Indians to hold more prominent positions in the nation's government.

The Festival of Empire in London lauded George and Mary's coronation ceremony at Westminster Abbey on June 22, 1911, when they were crowned as King and Queen. The King and Queen visited Ireland for five days in July, and they were welcomed with open arms. Many people lined the procession route to applaud them. The King and Queen traveled to India for the Delhi Durbar later that year, and on December 12, 1911, they were formally unveiled as the Emperor and Empress of India to a gathering of Indian authorities and nobles. At the event, George announced the transfer of the Indian capital from Calcutta to Delhi while donning the recently minted Imperial Crown of India. The only Indian Emperor who was accessible in his own Delhi Durbar was him. As he and Mary traveled the entire subcontinent, George decided to enjoy big game hunting in Nepal, where he spent more than 10 days taking down 21 tigers, 8 rhinoceroses, and a bear. He was a skilled and proficient marksman. George V detested modern art and detested taking portraits. He admired William Reid Dick, whose statue of George V is located outside Westminster Abbey in London, and Bertram Mackennal, who created sculptures of George for the display in Madras and Delhi.

Even though he and his better half occasionally traveled throughout the British Empire, George preferred to stay at home and pursue his hobbies of stamp collecting and game shooting. He also went about living an ordinary life that later biographers would find boring because to its routineness. He was not a learned man, as evidenced by his comment after returning after a night at the opera, "Went to Covent Garden and saw Fidelio and awful dull it was. He truly cared about Britain and the Commonwealth. He explained that it had always been my ambition to identify with the brilliant concept of the Empire. He demonstrated diligence and earned the respect of the British public. According to history expert David Cannadine, King George V and Queen Mary were an unmistakably committed pair who upheld moral principles. George established a code of conduct for British royalty that was modeled by the virtues and ideals of the upper working class rather than on the practices or vices of high society. He handled a series of crises, including those related to Ireland, World War I, and the socialist minority government in Britain, by acting within his legal bounds. He was a conservative by nature and never really embraced or approved of the forward-thinking changes taking place in British society. By the way, he consistently used his influence as a force for impartiality and balance, viewing his role as a middleman rather than an ultimate decision-maker.

Throughout the First World War, George's health deteriorated. At a troop inspection in France on October 28, 1915, his horse tossed him, severely injuring him, and his frequent smoking made his recurring breathing problems worse. He had bronchitis that persisted. On the doctors' advice, he was reluctantly sent on his final and third overseas trip since the war, a private cruise to the Mediterranean in 1925. His son Edward assumed many of his duties for the following two years as a result of his serious septicemia infection in November 1928. In 1929, the King "in rather a strong word" declined the invitation to take a longer holiday abroad. Instead, he chose to spend three months in retirement at Craigweil House in the Sussex seaside village of Aldwick. The Latin suffix Regis, which means "of the King," was given to the town as a result of his stay. When told he will soon be well enough to return to the town, it is said that his dying words were "Bugger Bognor!" George never fully recovered. In his final year, he occasionally received oxygen. When his favorite sister, Victoria, passed away in December 1935, he was heartbroken. On January 15, 1936, the King, who had a cold, went to his bedroom at Sandringham House and remained there until his demise. He was rapidly losing his stamina and was losing consciousness. Prime Minister Baldwin afterwards said: He had heard someone express gratitude for kindness every time he became aware that someone had been the object of a kind inquiry or observation. He did, however, ask his secretary, who had been called, in an unusually forthright way, "How is the Empire?" The King smiled and went back to sleep as the secretary said, "All is well, sir, with the Empire." By January 20, he had practically passed away. The King muttered "God damn you" as his final words. According to Dawson's secret diary, which was discovered after his death and made public in 1986, were directed at his nurse, Catherine Black, when she administered him a sedative that evening. The King's medical team, under the direction of Lord Dawson of Penn, released a report stating, "The King's life is moving quietly towards its close." Dawson, who supported the "gentle progression of euthanasia," admitted killing the King in the diary.

Around 11:00, it became apparent that the final stage might go on for several hours, unanticipated by the patient but failing to respect the dignity and peace that he so deeply deserved and which demanded a prompt resolution. When everything that is truly life has already died, waiting for the mechanical end for hours only exhausts the watchers and keeps them too agitated to appreciate the quiet of thought, community, or prayer. I then made the decision to find a remedy and injected cocaine grade 1 and morphine grade 3/4 into my engorged jugular vein. The physical exertion ends around a quarter of an hour later, with quieter breathing and a more relaxed attitude. Rather than in "less appropriate... evening journals," Dawson stated that the King's death at 11:55 p.m. may be reported in the morning edition of The Times newspaper. Dawson claimed that he made this decision to respect the King's dignity and to lessen the burden on the family. Both the extremely religious Queen Mary and the Prince of Wales, who might not have supported euthanasia, were not contacted. The King family opposed Dawson's actions while also not wanting the King to suffer or have his life unnaturally prolonged. The British Pathé network aired.

Part 2

Edward VIII

From 20 January 1936 until his abdication in December of that same year, Edward VIII (born Edward Albert Christian George Andrew Patrick David; 23 June 1894 – 28 May 1972) was both the Emperor of India and the King of the United Kingdom and the Dominions of the British Empire.

The oldest child of the Duke and Duchess of York, who would eventually become King George V and Queen Mary, Edward was born during the reign of his great-grandmother, Queen Victoria. His mother was the eldest child of Francis, Duke of Teck and Princess Mary Adelaide of Cambridge. He was third in line to the throne at the time of his birth, after his father and grandfather.

The Archbishop of Canterbury, Edward White Benson, christened him as Edward Albert Christian George Andrew Patrick David on July 16, 1894, in the Green Drawing Room of White Lodge. Prince Albert Victor, Duke of Clarence and Avondale, Edward's late uncle, was remembered by the name "Edward." who was referred to as "Eddy" within the family (Edward was one of his given names), "Albert" was added at the request of Queen Victoria for her late husband Albert, Prince Consort, "Christian" was added in memory of his great-grandfather King Christian IX of Denmark, and the final four names—George, Andrew, Patrick, and David—were inspired by, respectively, the patron saints of England,

Scotland, Ireland, and Wales. His family and close acquaintances usually referred to him by his last name, David. Even though he was a strict disciplinarian, Edward's father was obviously caring, and his mother showed a playful side to her kids that contrasted with her stern outward appearance. She found it amusing that the kids were playing a practical joke on their French teacher by putting tadpoles on toast, and she urged them to open up to her.

Edward and his younger siblings were raised by nannies rather than their parents, as was typical for upper-class kids at the time. Before Edward was to be brought to his parents, one of his early nannies would frequently abuse him by pinching him. The Duke and Duchess would send him and the nanny away as a result of his following sobbing and wails. After her abuse of the kids was revealed, the nanny was fired, and Charlotte Bill took her place. At first, Helen Bricka tutored Edward at home. After Queen Victoria died in 1901, his parents spent over nine months traveling the British Empire, but young Edward and his brothers stayed in Britain with his grandparents, Queen Alexandra and King Edward VII, who showered them with love.

After his parents left, Edward was left in the care of two men, Frederick Finch and Henry Hansell, who raised him and his siblings for the rest of their early years.

Hansell maintained Edward in his severe tutelage until he was about thirteen years old. He received private instruction in German and French. Edward passed the test required for admission to the Royal Naval College, Osborne, and enrolled there in 1907. Edward's father objected with Hansell's request for the prince to start school earlier. Edward spent two unsatisfying years at Osborne College before transferring to the Royal Naval College in Dartmouth. It was intended for the two-year program to be followed by enrollment in the Royal Navy.

On 6 May 1910, when his father succeeded to the throne as George V following the death of Edward VII, Edward automatically became Duke of Cornwall and Duke of Rothesay; a month later, on 23 June 1910, the day before his 16th birthday, he was made Prince of Wales and Earl of Chester. He started making serious plans for his upcoming reign as king. A keen horseman, he picked up the game of polo with the university club. He was withdrawn from his naval course before his formal graduation, served as a midshipman for three months aboard the battleship Hindustan, and then entered Magdalen College, Oxford, right away, after eight terms, he departed Oxford without receiving any academic credentials.

On July 13, 1911, at a special ceremony held at Caernarfon Castle, Edward was formally installed as Prince of Wales. Welsh politician David Lloyd George, Constable of the Castle and Chancellor of the Exchequer in the Liberal government, was responsible for the investiture. Edward was taught a few Welsh words by Lloyd George, who also created a pretty fantastical ritual in the form of a Welsh pageant. Edward had attained the legal age for military service when the First World War began in 1914, and he was eager to serve. Although Edward was willing to serve on the front lines after joining the Grenadier Guards in June 1914, Secretary of State for War Lord Kitchener refused to permit it, noting the severe harm that would result if the heir apparent to the crown were seized by the enemy. Despite this, Edward attended the front line as frequently as he could and saw trench combat firsthand, efforts for which he was given the Military Cross in 1916. Despite having a small part in the fight, he was well-liked by the combatants. He made his first flight for the military in 1918 and later earned his pilot's license.

Prince John, Edward's youngest brother, passed away on January 18, 1919, at the age of 13 due to a severe epileptic seizure. Edward, who was 11 years older than John and had hardly known him, viewed his death as "little more than a regrettable nuisance. He wrote to his mistress at the time that he had told her all about that little brother, and how he was an epileptic. John hasn't been seen by anyone other than the family in the last two years, and even then, it's only been sometimes. The unfortunate kid had more in common with animals than anything else. Additionally, he wrote his mother a hurtful letter, which has since been lost. He felt compelled to write her an apology letter, in which he declared "I feel such a cold-hearted and unsympathetic swine for writing all that I did... No one can realize more than you how little poor Johnnie meant to me who barely knew him... I feel so much for you, darling Mama, who was his mother." She didn't respond, but he felt obliged to write her an apology letter.

When he was at the height of his fame, he was the most photographed celebrity of the day and helped define men's fashion. According to Men's Wear magazine, during the Prince of Wales' visit to the United States in 1924, "the average young man in America is more interested in the clothes of the Prince of Wales than in any other person on earth." Despite his extensive travels, Edward held a common racial prejudice against foreigners and a majority of the Empire's subjects, thinking that whites were inherently superior. In 1920, during a trip to Australia, he wrote of the Indigenous Australians: "they are the most revolting form of living creatures I've ever seen!! They are the lowest known form of human beings & are the nearest thing to monkeys.

While on leave from his unit on the Western Front, Edward enjoyed spending his time having a good time in Paris. He met Marguerite Alibert, a Parisian courtesan, and fell in love with her. She preserved the frank letters he wrote her. After a year or so, Edward ended the relationship. Alibert fatally shot her husband in the Savoy Hotel in 1923, but she was exonerated in a sensational murder trial. The Royal Household fought tooth and nail to prevent any reference of Edward in relation to the trial or Alibert. In the 1920s and 1930s, Edward's womanizing and reckless behavior alarmed King George V, Prime Minister Stanley Baldwin, and those close to the prince.

In addition to being appalled by his son's affairs with married women and reluctance to see him succeed to the throne, George V was saddened by his son's incapacity to find true happiness in life. George predicted that the youngster would wreck himself in a year after his death.

Edward received a lease on Fort Belvedere in Windsor Great Park from George V in 1930. There, he continued to date a number of married women, including Freda Dudley Ward and Lady Furness, an American woman who was married to a British peer and who introduced the prince to Wallis Simpson, an American friend of hers. Simpson's first spouse, had been divorced, Win Spencer a naval lieutenant, in 1927. Businessman Ernest Simpson, her second husband, was of British and American descent. However, Edward's strained connection with his father was made worse by his friendship with Simpson. Although his parents had interacted with Simpson in 1935 at Buckingham Palace, they later declined to do so. Government and establishment elites were concerned about the possibility of an American divorcee with a dubious record having such influence over the heir apparent.

On January 20, 1936, King George V passed away, and Edward took the throne as King Edward VIII. The following day, with Simpson by his side, he defied tradition and watched the announcement of his own accession from a window of St. James's Palace. He made aviation history by flying from Sandringham to London for his Accession Council. He was the first monarch of the British Empire to do so. Edward's actions, which were perceived as meddling in political affairs, aroused uneasiness in government circles. Although he had not suggested any solution or change in policy, his remark that "something must be done" for the jobless coal miners on a tour of dismal areas in South Wales was perceived as an attempt to direct government policy. Because it was obvious that Edward was not paying attention to them, government ministers were hesitant to send private correspondence and official files to Fort Belvedere for fear that Simpson and other house guests may read them improperly or accidentally divulge state secrets. The currency that wore Edward's likeness also reflected his unconventional attitude to his duty. He defied the custom that each succeeding monarch's profile portrait face in the opposite way from that of his or her forebear. As his father had done, Edward insisted on turning his face away so that the part in his hair could be seen. Before the abdication, only a small number of test coins—all of which are extremely rare—were minted. In order to uphold tradition, George VI, who succeeded Edward as king, likewise faced left. This was done to imply that, had any additional coins with Edward's likeness been produced, they would have depicted him facing right. Edward and Simpson took the steam yacht Nahlin on a tour of the Eastern Mediterranean in August and September. By October, it was becoming obvious that the new monarch intended to wed Simpson, especially after the Simpsons filed for divorce at the Ipswich Assizes. Although there was a lot of rumors about his affair in the United States, the British media chose to remain silent, and until early December, the general public was in the dark.

Edward invited Prime Minister Stanley Baldwin to Buckingham Palace on November 16 and announced his intention to wed Simpson once she was free to remarry. Because the Church of England forbade second marriages after divorce, Baldwin advised him that his citizens would find the union morally repugnant and that they would not accept Simpson as queen. Edward served as the nominal leader of the Church, and the clergy looked on him to uphold its principles. Cosmo Gordon Lang, the Archbishop of Canterbury, was emphatic that Edward had to leave. A morganatic marriage, in which Edward would still be king but Simpson would not be the queen consort, was Edward's alternate proposal. Any children they might have would not inherit the kingdom, and she would instead enjoy a lesser title. Winston Churchill, a prominent politician, endorsed this in theory, and some historians contend that it was he who came up with the idea. In any case, the British Cabinet and other Dominion governments finally rejected it. The prime ministers of Australia Joseph Lyons, Canada Mackenzie King, and South Africa J. B. M. Hertzog made it clear that they opposed the king marrying a divorcee; while Éamon de Valera, the prime minister of Ireland, expressed indifference and detachment, and Michael Joseph Savage, the prime minister of New Zealand, who had never heard of Simpson before, vacillated in disbelief.

If he couldn't wed Simpson, Edward told Baldwin he would abdicate. Baldwin then gave Edward three choices: abandon the idea of marriage, wed against the advice of his ministers, or abdicate. It was obvious that Edward was unwilling to give up Simpson, and he was aware that if he wed against the counsel of his ministers, he would force the resignation of the government and spark a constitutional crisis. He decided to abdicate.

In the presence of his younger brothers Prince Albert, Duke of York, who was next in line to the throne, Prince Henry, Duke of Gloucester, and Prince George, Duke of Kent, Edward officially executed the documents of abdication at Fort Belvedere on December 10, 1936. The final act of his reign was the royal assent to His Majesty's Declaration of Abdication Act 1936, which stated that the monarch "declare my irrevocable determination to renounce the throne for myself and for my descendants and my desire that effect should be given to this instrument of abdication immediately.

All the Dominions had already given their approval to the abdication, as required by the Statute of Westminster. In a worldwide BBC radio broadcast on the evening of December 11, 1936, Edward—now adopting the title and manners of a prince—explained his decision to abdicate. The decision was "mine and mine alone... The other person most nearly concerned has tried up to the last to persuade me to take a different course," he said, adding that "I have found it impossible to carry the heavy burden of responsibility and to discharge my duties as I would wish to do without the help and support of the woman I love." Edward left Britain for Austria the next day; he was unable to join Simpson until her divorce became final.

As a result of his brother's accession to the throne as George VI, Princess Elizabeth, George VI's elder daughter, became the presumed heir.

George VI declared his intention to create his brother as the "Duke of Windsor" with the title of Royal Highness on December 12, 1936, at the Privy Council of the United Kingdom's accession meeting. He wanted this to be his first official act as king, even though the official papers weren't signed until March 8, 1937. Edward was recognized as the Duke of Windsor in the meantime.

Less than a month before his 78th birthday, on May 28, 1972, the Duke passed away at his house in Paris, ten days following the Queen's visit. His remains were brought back to Britain and are now entombed at St. George's Chapel in Windsor Castle. The Duchess of Windsor, who was visiting and stayed at Buckingham Palace, as well as the Queen and other members of the royal family, attended the funeral service on June 5 in the chapel. He was laid to rest in the Royal Burial Ground at Frogmore, which is located behind the Royal Mausoleum of Queen Victoria and Prince Albert. Up until a 1965 royal agreement, the Duke and Duchess had intended to be buried in a plot they had acquired in Baltimore's Green Mount Cemetery.

where the Duchess's father was buried. Frail and developing dementia, the Duchess passed away in 1986 and was laid to rest next to her husband.

Part 3

George VI

On 11 December 1936 until his passing in 1952, (Albert Frederick Arthur George; 14 December 1895 – 6 February 1952) ruled the United Kingdom and the Dominions of the British Commonwealth. Prior to the British Raj's dissolution in August 1947, he served as India's final emperor. The king George VI was born during the reign of his great-grandmother Queen Victoria; he was given the name Albert at birth in honor of his great-grandfather Albert, Prince Consort. To his family and close associates, he was known simply as "Bertie."

During the reign of his great-grandmother Queen Victoria, George VI was born at York Cottage on the Sandringham Estate in Norfolk. The Queen was comforted by the suggestion to name the new baby Albert and wrote to the Duchess of York: "I am all impatience to see the new one, born on such a sad day but rather more dear to me, especially as he will be called by that dear name which is a byword for all that is great and good."

His father was Prince George, Duke of York (later King George V). As a result, on February 17, 1896, he was baptized at St. Mary Magdalene Church in Sandringham as "Albert Frederick Arthur George." Despite going by "Bertie" in the family, His Highness Prince Albert of York was his official title. At the time of his birth, Albert was fourth in line to the throne, behind his grandfather, father, and elder brother.

In addition to being frequently ill, Albert was also noted for being "easily frightened and somewhat prone to weeping." He stammered, and it lasted for years. He was obliged to write with his right hand because it was customary at the time, despite the fact that he is naturally left-handed.

He suffered from recurring stomach issues and had knock knees for which he needed to wear uncomfortable splints.

Albert enrolled as a navy cadet at the Royal Naval College, Osborne, beginning in 1909. He performed poorly on the final exam in 1911, yet he nevertheless advanced to the Royal Naval College, Dartmouth. His father became King George V after the passing of his grandfather, Edward VII, in 1910. Albert was second in line to the throne, thus Edward was made Prince of Wales.

On the training ship HMS Cumberland, Albert spent the first half of 1913 in the West Indies and along Canada's east coast. On September 15, 1913, he was rated as a midshipman aboard HMS Collingwood. He was in the Mediterranean for three months, but he was never able to get over his seasickness. He was medically evacuated from the ship to Aberdeen three weeks after the start of World War I, where Sir John Marnoch removed his appendix. He was acknowledged in dispatches for his performance as a turret commander on Collingwood during the Battle of Jutland, the pivotal naval engagement of the war, which took place between May 31 and June 1, 1916. He did not participate in any more action, primarily because to health issues brought on by a duodenal ulcer for which he underwent surgery in November 1917.

The historian R. V. Laurence served as Albert's "formal tutor" while he attended Trinity College in Cambridge, where he studied history, economics, and civics for a year. His father gave him the titles of Duke of York, Earl of Inverness, and Baron Killarney on June 4 of that year. He started doing more royal responsibilities. He traveled to coal mines, industries, and rail yards in the place of his father. Through these trips, he earned the name "Industrial Prince." He appeared less self-assured in public than his older brother, Edward, due to his stammer, his shame over it, and a propensity for shyness. Nevertheless, he was fit and he liked to play tennis. In 1926, he competed in the Men's Doubles at Wimbledon alongside Louis Greig, losing in the opening round. He became interested in working conditions and served as the Industrial Welfare Society's president.

Albert's ability to choose a potential wife with such independence was exceptional at a time when royalty was supposed to wed other royalty. In April 1920, the King convinced Albert to break up with Lady Loughborough, an Australian socialite who was already married, by offering him the dukedom of York. He had not seen Lady Elizabeth Bowes-Lyon since childhood until that year. She was the youngest child of Claude Bowes-Lyon, the 14th Earl of Strathmore, and King Horne. He made up his mind to wed her. Elizabeth reportedly turned down his proposal twice, in 1921 and 1922, as a result of her reluctance to make the sacrifices required to join the royal family. The choice of his wife would "make or mar" Albert, according to Cecilia Bowes-Lyon, Countess of Strathmore and King Horne.

Elizabeth finally consented to marry him after a protracted courting. On April 26, 1923, Albert and Elizabeth were wed in Westminster Abbey. Albert feared speaking in front of crowds because of his stammer. He started seeing Australian-born speech therapist Lionel Logue after his concluding address at the British Empire Exhibition at Wembley on October 31, 1925, which was a test for both him and his audience.

The Duchess carefully practiced breathing techniques with Logue while the Duke and Logue did so. He was then able to speak more freely after that. During a tour across the empire in 1927 with the Duchess, the Duke opened the new Parliament House in Canberra, Australia, with an enhanced delivery. They traveled by ship from Jamaica to Australia, New Zealand, and Fiji. Albert played doubles tennis with Bertrand Clark, which was unique at the time and was interpreted locally as a sign of racial equality.

The family referred to the Duke and Duchess' two children as "Lilibet", Elizabeth who was born in 1926, and Margaret, who was born in 1930. 145 Piccadilly was the home of the close-knit family, not one of the royal palaces. "After I am dead, the lad will wreck himself in twelve months," the king said of Prince Edward. "I hope God that my eldest son will never marry and that nothing will stand between Bertie and Lilibet and the crown," he added.

Albert was the presumed heir to the throne because Edward was single and had no children. In less than a year, on December 11, 1936, Edward abdicated the throne in order to wed Wallis Simpson, who was divorcing both her first and second husbands. British Prime Minister Stanley Baldwin had warned Edward that he could not continue to be king and wed a woman who had been divorced and had two surviving ex-husbands. Albert, who had been hesitant to take the throne, succeeded him after his abdication. Albert visited his mother, Queen Mary, in London the day before the abdication. When he informed her what had happened, he noted in his diary, "I broke down and sobbed like a child."

The rumor that Albert was incapable of being king on both a physical and psychological level grew throughout Britain. There is no proof to back up the contemporary story that the government considered choosing their younger brother George, Duke of Kent, over him, his children, and his brother Henry. Given that George was the only brother with a son at the time, it appears that this was proposed. The uncertainty surrounding his predecessor and brother's titles, manners, and positions dominated the early years of George VI's rule. Although George VI believed that Edward had forfeited his right to use royal titles, including "Royal Highness," by abdicating and relinquishing the succession, he had been introduced as "His Royal Highness Prince Edward" for the abdication broadcast. George's first move as king was to give his brother the title "Duke of Windsor" and the style "Royal Highness" in order to resolve the matter, but the letters patent establishing the dukedom forbade any wife or children from having royal styles. Due to the fact that Balmoral Castle and Sandringham House were private residences and did not belong to the crown, George VI was forced to purchase them from Edward The day that Edward's coronation was originally scheduled for, May 12, 1937, actually saw the crowning of George VI at Westminster Abbey. In a departure from custom, his mother Queen Mary showed support for her son by showing up to the wedding. As it had done for his father, George VI's Durbar was not held in Delhi since the cost would have been borne by the Government of India.

The early years of George VI's reign were dominated by the escalating threat of war in Europe. The King was required by the constitution to assist Prime Minister Neville Chamberlain's efforts to pacify Hitler. The United Kingdom and the self-governing Dominions other than Ireland declared war on Nazi Germany in response to the German invasion of Poland in September 1939.

Despite German air raids, George VI and his wife made the decision to remain in London. Although they frequently stayed the night at Windsor Castle, they were formally housed in Buckingham Palace throughout the duration of the war. On September 7, 1940, the first night of the London Blitz claimed the lives of around a thousand people, principally in the East End. On September 13, while the King and Queen were at Buckingham Palace, two German bombs detonated in a courtyard, just missing them. The Queen reacted angrily, saying, "I am pleased we have been bombed. It gives me hope that we can confront the East End. The royal family was depicted as experiencing the same perils and hardships as the rest of the nation. The Duke of Kent, the King's brother, died while serving in August 1942.

Winston Churchill succeeded Neville Chamberlain as prime minister in 1940, but George personally would have chosen Lord Halifax. The King and Churchill established "the closest personal relationship in modern British history between a monarch and a prime minister" after the King's initial disappointment at Churchill's choice of Lord Beaverbrook to the Cabinet. The two men had lunch alone and talked frankly and covertly about the conflict. The only surviving first-person account of these meetings is in the King's diary, which contains most of what the two talked about. The King and Queen made morale-boosting visits to troops, weapons factories, and bomb sites around the United Kingdom throughout the war.

Their prominent public personas and what appeared to be unwavering resolve earned them a place as icons of the country's resistance. Field Marshal Alan Brooke, the Chief of the Imperial General Staff, admitted that he believed Field Marshal Bernard Montgomery was pursuing his position every time they met at a social event in 1944. You should be concerned because whenever I meet him, I always assume he's after mine, the King retorted. The King's health had suffered due to the strain of the war, which was made worse by his habitual smoking, which led to the development of lung cancer among other illnesses like arteriosclerosis and Buerger's disease. After the King underwent a right lumbar sympathectomy in March 1949 to relieve an arterial blockage in his right leg that threatened to result in the loss of the leg, a tour to Australia and New Zealand that had been scheduled was cancelled. The heir apparent's older daughter Elizabeth assumed greater regal responsibilities as her father's health declined. The King traveled to the London Airport on January 31, 1952, against the advice of those close to him, to see Elizabeth and Philip off on their tour to Australia via Kenya. It was his final outing in public. At 7:30 GMT on February 6th, six days later, he was discovered dead in bed at Sandringham House in Norfolk. He had passed away at the age of 56 during the night from a coronary thrombosis. As Queen Elizabeth II, his daughter took a flight from Kenya to the United Kingdom.

The coffin of George VI was at rest in St. Mary Magdalene Church in Sandringham from February 9 until it was placed in state at Westminster Hall on February 11. On the fifteenth, he was laid to rest in St. George's Chapel at Windsor Castle. He was initially buried in the Royal Vault before being moved on March 26, 1969, to the King George VI Memorial Chapel inside St. George's. In 2002, fifty years after his passing, his younger daughter Princess Margaret's ashes and the remains of his widow, Queen Elizabeth the Queen Mother, who both passed away that year, were buried next to him in the chapel.

36

Part 4

Elizabeth II

On 6 February 1952 until her passing on 8 September 2022, Elizabeth Alexandra Mary reigned over the United Kingdom and the other Commonwealth realms. She held the title of monarch in 15 of the 32 sovereign states where she governed as queen regnant during her lifetime. She has the longest recorded reign of any female head of state in history, at 70 years and 214 days, and the longest of any British monarch. Elizabeth was the first child born to the Duke and Duchess of York and was born in Mayfair, London (later King George VI and Queen Elizabeth). Elizabeth was the presumed heir when her father assumed the throne in 1936 following the abdication of his brother, King Edward VIII.

Elizabeth was born on April 21, 1926, while her paternal grandfather, King George V, was in power. The second son of the King was her father, Prince Albert, Duke of York (later King George VI). Elizabeth Bowes-Lyon, Duchess of York, later known as Queen Elizabeth the Queen Mother, was born by Caesarean section at the London residence of her father, Scottish aristocracy Claude Bowes-Lyon, 14th Earl of Strathmore and King Horne (17 Bruton Street, Mayfair). In the private chapel of Buckingham Palace, she was baptized on May 29 by the Anglican Archbishop of York, Cosmo Gordon Lang. She was given the names Elizabeth after her mother, Alexandra after her paternal great-grandmother, who had passed away six months earlier, and Mary after her paternal grandmother. She was adored by her grandfather, George V, whom she adoringly referred to as "Grandpa England," and her regular visits during his serious illness in 1929 were credited in the popular press and by later biographers with lifting his spirits and assisting his recovery. She was known as "Lilibet" by her close family, based on what she initially called herself. Princess Margaret, Elizabeth's only sibling, was born in 1930. The two princesses received their education at home under the guidance of their mother and Marion Crawford, their governess.

Elizabeth was third in line for the British throne during her grandfather's reign, after her father and her uncle Edward. Even though her birth sparked curiosity in the public, it was not anticipated that she would become queen because Edward was still a child and was most likely to be married and have his own children, who would succeed Elizabeth in the line of succession.

She passed her father to take the place of her uncle as heir apparent after the death of her grandfather in 1936. After his anticipated union with divorced socialite Wallis Simpson sparked a constitutional crisis later that year, Edward abdicated. As a result, George VI, Elizabeth's father, ascended to the throne. Elizabeth became the presumed successor because she didn't have any brothers. Elizabeth studied constitutional history privately with Vice-Provost Henry Marten of Eton College, and she also took French lessons from a string of native-speaking governesses. The 1st Buckingham Palace Company of the Girl Guides was established especially for her to interact with other girls her age. She afterwards joined the Sea Rangers. Up until Christmas 1939, the princesses resided at Scotland's Balmoral Castle before relocating to Norfolk's Sandringham House.

Elizabeth, at 14 years old, addressed other kids who had been evacuated from the cities in her first radio transmission, which she made in 1940 as part of the BBC's Children's Hour. She remarked: "In addition to trying to shoulder our fair part of the peril and sorrow of war, we are doing everything we can to support our brave sailors, soldiers, and airmen. Every single one of us is aware that everything will work out in the end." In order for her to serve as one of the five Counsellors of State in the event of her father's disability or absence abroad, such as during his trip to Italy in July 1944, parliament altered the statute as she got closer to turning 18 years old. She was given the service number 230873 and appointed an honorary second subaltern in the Auxiliary Territorial Service in February 1945. Five months after completing her training as a technician and driver, she was promoted to honorary junior commander, the female equivalent of captain at the time. On Victory in Europe Day, which marked the conclusion of the European War, Elizabeth and Margaret mingled covertly with the revelers in the streets of London.

She should become Princess of Wales when she turns 18 years old, according to Welsh MPs. The King disagreed, believing that such a title belonged only to the wife of a

Prince of Wales, who had always been the heir apparent. The notion was supported by Home Secretary Herbert Morrison. At the National Eisteddfod of Wales in 1946, she was admitted to the Gorsedd of Bards.

In 1947, Princess Elizabeth traveled to her first foreign country with her parents, touring southern Africa. "I declare before you all that my whole life, whether it be long or short, shall be committed to your service and the service of our great imperial family, to which we all belong," she said in a broadcast to the British Commonwealth on the occasion of her 21st birthday during the visit.

Dermot Morrah, a journalist for The Times, wrote the speech. Elizabeth first met Prince Philip of Greece and Denmark in 1934, and they reconnected in 1937. They were third cousins through Queen Victoria and second cousins once removed through King Christian IX of Denmark. Elizabeth, who was only 13 at the time, claimed she fell in love with Philip after their third encounter at the Royal Naval College in Dartmouth in July 1939. They then started writing to one another. When their engagement was formally announced on July 9, 1947, she was 21 years old. The relationship was not without controversy because Philip had no money, was foreign-born (despite being a British national who had fought in the Royal Navy during World War II), and had sisters who had wed Nazi-affiliated German noblemen. Prior to being married, Philip gave up his Greek and Danish titles, made a formal conversion from Greek

Orthodoxy to Anglicanism, took the name Lieutenant Philip Mountbatten, the British surname of his mother's family, and assumed the style of Lieutenant Philip Mountbatten.

He received the title of His Royal Highness and the title of Duke of Edinburgh just before the wedding. At Westminster Abbey, Elizabeth and Philip exchanged vows on November 20, 1947. On November 14, 1948, Elizabeth gave birth to Prince Charles, her first child. The King had granted letters of patent to her children a month earlier, allowing them to adopt the title and style of a royal prince or princess, to which they would not have otherwise been entitled since their father was no longer a royal prince. Princess Anne was born on August 15, 1950, as the second child. After getting hitched, the couple rented Windlesham Moor, a property close to Windsor Castle, until July 1949, when they moved into Clarence House in London.

Elizabeth and Philip left for Australia and New Zealand at the beginning of 1952, traveling through Kenya. They had barely gotten back to Sagana Lodge in Kenya on February 6, 1952, after spending the previous night at Treetops Hotel, when word of George VI's passing and Elizabeth's subsequent ascension to the throne with immediate effect reached them. The new queen received the news from Philip. Since she was the first Elizabeth to rule Scotland, many Scots were angered by her use of the name Elizabeth II as her regnal name. She was crowned queen over all of her realms, and the royal party hurried back to the UK. Philip and Elizabeth settled into Buckingham Palace. Following the tradition of a wife assuming her husband's surname upon marriage, it was likely with Elizabeth's accession that the royal house would bear the Duke of Edinburgh's name. The House of Mountbatten moniker was promoted by Lord Mountbatten. The House of Edinburgh was Philip's idea, in honor of his ducal title. Elizabeth said on April 9, 1952, that the House of Windsor will continue to be the name of the royal house in support of Winston Churchill, the British prime minister, and Elizabeth's grandmother, Queen Mary. "I am the only individual in the country who isn't allowed to give his name to his offspring," the Duke griped. The surname Mountbatten-Windsor was chosen in 1960 for the male line descendants of Philip and Elizabeth who do not hold royal titles.

Queen Mary passed away on 24 March 1953, but the coronation took place as scheduled on 2 June, as Mary had ordered before she passed away. With the exception of the anointing and communion, the coronation in Westminster Abbey was broadcast on television for the first time. Elizabeth requested that the floral symbols of the Commonwealth nations be stitched on her coronation gown. Elizabeth rarely participated in interviews, and little is known about her innermost thoughts. She did not clearly state her political ideas in a public setting, and it is improper to inquire about or make public the monarch's opinions.

Elizabeth took her Coronation Oath seriously and had a strong sense of civic and religious obligation. She worshiped with the national Church of Scotland in addition to her official position as Supreme Governor of the established Church of England. She expressed her support for interreligious dialogue and met with five popes, including Pius XII, John XXIII, John Paul II, Benedict XVI, and Francis. In the 1950s, Elizabeth was portrayed as a dazzling "fairytale Queen" when she was a young woman at the beginning of her reign. After the horrors of World War II, it was a moment of optimism, a time of advancement and success that heralded a "new Elizabethan age." It was a very uncommon remark when Lord Altrincham claimed in 1957 that her words resembled those of a "priggish schoolgirl." By broadcasting Prince Charles' inauguration as Prince of Wales and the television documentary Royal Family in the late 1960s, attempts were made to provide a more contemporary image of the monarchy. Her clothing evolved into a recognizable, distinctive look that was more about utility than fashion. She wore clothing with an emphasis on what was appropriate rather than fashionable. She started out wearing largely solid-colored overcoats and hats in public so that she could stand out in a crowd. A team of five dressers, a dressmaker, and a milliner took care of her clothes. The crowds and festivities for Elizabeth's Silver Jubilee in 1977 were truly joyful; nevertheless, as the private and professional lives of Elizabeth's children came under media scrutiny in the 1980s, popular criticism of the royal family grew. In the 1990s, her popularity hit a low point. She started paying income tax for the first time as a result of public pressure, and Buckingham Palace was made public. Although republican ideology was still a minority point of view and Elizabeth herself enjoyed excellent approval ratings, support for republicanism in Britain appeared to be higher than it had ever been in recent memory. Instead of Elizabeth herself, criticism was directed at the monarchy as a whole and the behavior of Elizabeth's extended family. Although Elizabeth's popularity—as well as support for the monarchy in general—rose after her live television broadcast to the entire globe five days after Diana's passing, discontent with the monarchy peaked on the day of the Princess of Wales's death. Elizabeth was the sovereign of numerous orders in her own countries, held numerous titles and honorary military positions across the Commonwealth, and she was honored and decorated internationally. She was referred to as the Lord of Mann and the Duke of Normandy, respectively. Defender of the Faith and Duke of Lancaster are further fashions. It was customary to address Elizabeth as Your Majesty before calling her Ma'am while speaking with her.

Following concerns from doctors, Buckingham Palace declared on September 8, 2022, Queen Elizabeth was receiving medical attention at Balmoral Castle. The declaration said, "Following more testing this morning, Elizabeth's doctors have expressed worry for Her Majesty's health and advised that she continue to be under close observation. The Queen stays put in Balmoral in comfort." In addition to her daughters-in-law and grandchildren Prince William and Prince Harry, Elizabeth's four children also made the trip to Balmoral. That evening around 18:30 BST, her passing was officially announced, launching Operation London Bridge and Operation Unicorn because she passed away in Scotland.

Conclusion

Charles Philip Arthur George, born on November 14, 1948, was formally installed as the monarch of Great Britain on September 10, 2022, in a ceremony rooted in historical precedent and social symbolism that was televised live for the first time. When his mother, Queen Elizabeth II, passed away on Thursday, Charles immediately ascended to the throne. However, the accession ceremony is a significant constitutional and ceremonial step in introducing the new monarch to the nation.

Numerous prominent leaders from the past and present without Charles, legally establishing his title, King Charles III.

"I know how strongly you and the entire nation, and I guess I may say the whole world, grieve with me in this irreparable loss we have all endured," he said, expressing his own sorrow. The day of his mother's funeral was declared a public holiday by the new monarch, Although the state funeral's date has not been made public at that point in time, it is anticipated to occur around September 19.

www.ingramcontent.com/pod-product-compliance
Lightning Source LLC
Chambersburg PA
CBHW051712250726

48653CB00007B/2998